The Art of Doing Nothing

By Véronique Vienne with photographs by Erica Lennard

The Art of Doing Nothing

SIMPLE WAYS TO MAKE TIME FOR YOURSELF

Clarkson Potter/Publishers
New York

Published by Clarkson N. Potter, Inc., 201 East 50th Street, New York, New York 10022.
Member of the Crown Publishing Group.

Random House, Inc. New York, Toronto, London, Sydney, Auckland
www.randomhouse.com

CLARKSON N. POTTER, POTTER, and colophon are trademarks of Clarkson N. Potter, Inc.

Printed in Japan

Design by Skouras Design

Library of Congress Cataloging-in-Publication Data
Vienne, Véronique.
The art of doing nothing / by Véronique Vienne ; photographs by Erica Lennard.—1st ed.
Includes bibliographical references.
1. Stress (Psychology). 2. Stress management. 3. Relaxation. I. Title.
BF575.S75V55   1998
155.9'042—dc21   97–30497

ISBN 0-609-60074-5

10   9   8   7   6

DEDICATION

To the spirit of Mount Tamalpais

ACKNOWLEDGMENTS

This book would not have been possible without our agent, Helen Forson Pratt, who brought us together, and without our editor, Annetta Hanna, who believed that a book about nothing could turn into something. Special thanks to Sharona Jones, for her help in research, and to Irene Silvagni, Lise Ryall, Ann Rhoney, Kazuko, and Claudia Van Rysen, for providing inspiration for the photographs. We are also indebted to our husbands, Bill Young and Denis Colomb, who have taught us the value of slowing down.

CONTENTS

Ah! To do nothing—and do it well.

Whenever friends or loved ones kindly suggest we relax—take a deep breath or unwind for a few days—we almost always protest. Slowing down takes too much time. A generation of doers, we have dedicated our lives to making things happen. We feel, quite rightly, that there is nothin' we can't do—except, of course, doing nothing.

For us, being in a state of not-doing is the outer edge, the ultimate luxury, the impossible dream. But could it be that we've been looking for that elusive nothing in all the wrong places?

Peace of mind is not a rare and exotic flower that only blooms on deserted islands or on top of mountains. You don't have to travel far and wide to find it. Relaxation is actually a native plant that grows in your own backyard—a hardy one at that. It never

entirely gives up, although we repeatedly try to uproot it.

This book is designed to help you cultivate the seeds of serenity. In your everyday life. While you breathe. Or listen. Or wait. In the course of a meal or in the middle of a traffic jam. When you rush to catch a plane or when you are afraid to miss a deadline.

Surely, *you* don't have to be lectured about the benefits of rest and relaxation. Your mind, on the other hand, must be cajoled. You must reason with your reason to convince it that it is in its own best interest to let go of its grip—from time to time.

If you don't prevail upon your brain, you will feel guilty whenever you put your feet up. So read on. With a little luck, you will find in these pages the arguments you need to sweet-talk yourself into a lull.

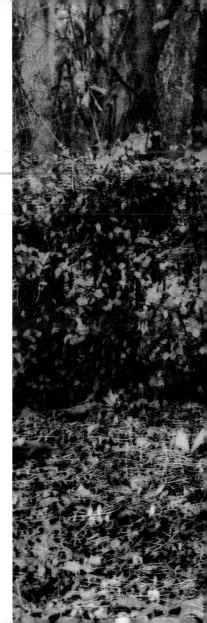

1

the art of
procrastinating

When confronted with a flat surface—stone, ice, or glass—water always meanders. Even when there are no obstructions, a fluid will invariably take the roundabout approach. One of the most plentiful compounds on earth, water is also the single largest constituent of our bodies. The world is 70 percent water—and so are we. It should come as no surprise, then, that human beings tend to dillydally as soon

10

as they are in a pressure-free environment. For us, as for most living organisms in nature, the path of least resistance is a succession of languid curves.

Procrastination is innate. It is an invisible force that drives rivers into serpentine patterns, underwater currents into sinuous paths, jet streams into winding courses—and you and me into a rambling mode.

What purpose these convolutions serve, no one knows. For instance, we understand how the Mississippi meanders, but we don't know *why*. To be sure, there are, for people at least, definite advantages to meandering.

For one thing, it takes you places you would otherwise have missed. It also gets you to do things that are long overdue. Instead of paying bills, for example, you decide to organize your sock drawer. Rather than fix the garage door, you give the new puppy a bath. How about working on your novel? First you want to strip the waxy buildup off the kitchen floor. Maybe procrastinating is nature's way of tidying up messes and cleaning up corners.

Too bad most of us postpone goofing off until Saturday or Sunday. In doing so, we put pressure on the weekend. Procrastinating on schedule creates yet another form of obligation. So try to waste time on the spur of the moment, on a Wednesday or a Thursday. Later—much later—when you get the hang of it, you'll be able to show off and fritter time away on a Monday.

Also, begin your procrastinating practice at home. Learn to vagabond between four walls before you venture outdoors. And because decelerating involves quite a lot of zigzagging and bouncing up and down, be sure to wear athletic shoes in order to get enough traction.

Choose an innocent project at first, like sorting out the magazines strewn near your bed. Stop to read the last paragraph of any

Lead me up the garden path.

Going with the flow: Indian youth watching the incoming monsoon.

out the window, fluff pillows, write in your journal, or brush your teeth.

Give yourself permission to abandon any activity midway. Welcome the urge to check whether the vacuum cleaner needs a new bag. Don't worry—you probably will never make it to the broom closet. Somewhere down the hallway, you will lose interest. Ten minutes later, you'll find yourself rummaging through your collection of postcards, looking for the one you wrote in Italy but never mailed because the post office went on strike.

While you poke along, the thought of phone calls to return, thank-you notes to write, errands to run, and money to make will probably haunt you. Dig in your heels. Take advantage of the squeegee action of your non-skid sneakers to resist the temptation to buzz, fuss, and bustle.

An hour of procrastination is equivalent to an hour at the gym. Granted, dragging your

article that looks interesting. Don't get sanguine, though. Interrupt yourself to glance

feet looks a lot easier than lifting weights. But don't let appearances deceive you. Repressing productive impulses is just as much of a workout as indulging them. Like low-impact isometric exercises that involve very small muscle contractions but result in a marked increase in muscle tone, working against the relentless pressure of our self-imposed guilt can burn a lot of calories.

To test this theory, stand next to a big pile of unopened mail. Decide not to rummage through it. Maybe it contains the refund check you have been expecting or a dreaded notice of termination from your cable company. So what. No envelope, please.

Feel the tension in your body as you hesitate. Just a peek? Don't give in. As you hold out, consider the following: Not opening your mail is tantamount to arm wrestling with one of the most powerful gravitational forces in the universe—the Puritan Work Ethic.

IN THE FOOTSTEPS OF THOREAU

By taking procrastination out of the home and into the woods, Henry David Thoreau helped make idleness part of the American cult of nature. "When I go out of the house for a walk, uncertain as yet whither I will bend my steps," wrote the celebrated resident of Walden Pond, "[I] submit myself to my instinct to decide for me."

Unlike Sierra Club founder John Muir, famous for his vigorous thousand-mile hike from Indiana to the Gulf Coast, Thoreau preferred to ramble aimlessly in the wilderness, a distracted pilgrim in search of leafy sanctuaries. "The walking of which I speak has nothing in it akin to exercise," he offered.

Two or three hours of capricious meandering would carry him to "as strange a country as I ever expect to see." This approach to walking was what Thoreau called sauntering, a technique he believed was used by French errant knights (the French *sans terre* means "without land or home"). Itinerant warriors, these freelance saunterers were always on the move, journeying from castle to castle, in search of their next crusade or military assignment.

Like Thoreau, who was a self-proclaimed advocate of voluntary poverty, the medieval Don Quixotes lived hand-to-mouth— rewarded for their services with gifts in kind. In the Middle Ages, cash was a rare commodity. With barter a way of life, procrastination was popular with everyone from kings to beggars.

Making money is a relatively new invention—something feudal lords stumbled upon eight hundred years ago when they discovered, quite by chance, that their idle servants looked a lot happier when they had less free time, more work to do, and the prospect of a few gold coins as a reward.

It is a sad commentary on human nature, but people in general prefer to toil from nine to five rather than get busy every now and then with waiting periods in between.

The new money economy in the twelfth century heralded the beginning of modern times, and the end of the meandering age. Yet, today, with a little imagination, you can still saunter in Thoreau's footsteps— whether you choose to go fishing or decide to play hooky and catch a matinee at the movies.

Don't let mercenary activities take over your life. Poke along, once in a while. Show the feudal establishment that there is more to the pursuit of happiness than a job description, a rigid schedule, and a fat paycheck.

whistling 101

"You know how to whistle, don't you?" said Bacall to Bogart.
"Just purse your lips and blow."

Want to take some pressure off yourself or let the air out of a tense situation? Try whistling a few notes. If you are not a born whistler, here is what else you need to know:

- Purse your lips and blow—but don't expect to make a note quite yet.
- Imitate the sound of the wind under a door. Do that for a while.
- Practice adjusting the shape of your lips. The smaller the hole, the higher the note will be.
- As soon as you get a sound—any sound—try to warble by moving your tongue up and down as you blow.
- Resist the temptation to put pressure on your breath in order to get a tone.
- Hear a tune in your head and improvise on it. Have fun; don't worry about how good or bad you sound.

You feel pretty sexy and carefree with your puckered lips, don't you? Hold on to that feeling. Soon you'll be whistling Dixie.

the art of breathing

irds do it. Bees do it. We do it. We exhale and release into the atmosphere carbon dioxide, a chemical that promotes the growth of plants and prevents the sun's radiant energy from returning to space. With our breath, we keep the planet from becoming a desert.

Apparently, one of our functions on this earth is to be gardeners—unwitting caretakers of a fragile

ecosystem. We may be detrimental to the environment in other ways, but when we empty our lungs, we help make the grass grow greener.

For some reason, in our culture, there is a lot more emphasis on inhaling than on exhaling. While we associate taking in oxygen with doing something useful and good for ourselves, we expel carbon dioxide surreptitiously, almost as if we were taking out the garbage—in a rush, nose pinched, mouth open. Always on the uptake, we derive almost no pleasure from relaxing our chests, clearing our airways, and sending forth some colorless CO_2 into the blue yonder.

To breathe deeply and effortlessly, don't wait to exhale. Think of breathing as giving, not taking. Just tell yourself that you are going to fill up your lungs *in order to* expel as much air as possible. Don't scrimp. Dole out an ample supply of car-bon dioxide. Do your share to promote photosynthesis. Picture in your mind one of your favorite trees and give its leaves a chance to produce some grade-A, top-quality oxygen.

Before you know it, your chest swells, your thoracic cage enlarges, and your shoulders relax. Precisely at the moment when you would expect your pulmonary chamber to be filled to capacity, the lobes in the back of your lungs open up like tiny parachutes. It is the most effortless high you've experienced in a long time—but it's nothing compared with the delicious sinking feeling that's yours when you exhale. Few things in life are as satisfying as this long, gentle dive into serenity.

It's wise never to urge yourself to breathe deeply: The involuntary mechanism that regulates the swapping of chemicals between our blood and the atmosphere is triggered by a series of very complex neuro-

Picture in your mind one of your favorite trees.

logical responses to internal and external stimuli. The central controls for respiration are in the brain, so changing the way we think about breathing is more effective than forcing the rib cage to expand.

It's all in your head. Mental images will affect breathing patterns more than abdominal lifts, diaphragm contractions, nostril-intensive yoga exercises, or hits of oxygen taken at trendy ozone bars.

When you breathe a sigh of relief, it's your body smiling.

BREATHING AND PAIN CONTROL

Although there is no scientific evidence that speeding up the removal of carbon dioxide from the bloodstream relieves pain, the medical profession insists on telling patients to take a deep breath before proceeding with unpleasant, intrusive, or possibly embarrassing probes. Whenever doctors say, "Now, take a deep breath," we tense up. We know (and our physicians know we know) that whatever they are up to is going to hurt. But being docile, we all submit and inhale bravely—teeth clenched and muscles rigid with repressed anxiety.

A folk remedy against pain, the take-a-deep-breath routine is in fact a visualizing exercise. As our chests heave, we are conditioned to imagine the pain being drawn up into the lungs and expelled through the mouth and nose.

And why not? It is quite possible that the oxygen-rich lung area—a big sponge with a blotting surface equal to that of a spacious two-bedroom apartment—can actually mop up physiological tensions and dissolve them into the atmosphere with each exhalation.

While alternative medicine puts its faith in the analgesic power of the breath, conventional medicine believes only in its distracting action and prescribes deep breathing as something that takes a patient's mind away from the pain. The result is the same: Quick exhales come in handy when you are in physical distress. It's a fact: Women who have used the Lamaze method of childbirth have found that panting is most soothing during periods of extreme strain.

If the throbbing gets worse, don't hesitate to moan, whimper, and wail—it's all part of letting the air out of the lungs.

In classic Greek drama, there was always a chorus of actors ready to lament and grieve. Their role was to express the fears of ordinary people in the face of tragedy. With their groans, they encouraged spectators to experience a catharsis—that healing sense of renewal that comes from releasing tensions.

When a crisis is over, breathe a sigh of relief. The murmur of the breath as it gently passes through the vocal cords makes for the sweetest ending.

A measure of happiness is how often we sigh with ease.

Staying in the Moment

Paying attention to the breath is like walking on the tightrope that links our conscious minds to the unconscious universe. Try it and experience the heady vertigo of mindfulness. But watch your step—it's not easy to stay up in the here and now of self-awareness.

- ❋ Stand by a window and look toward the horizon to minimize visual distractions.

- ❋ Note how shallow your first breaths are—but resist the temptation to increase the volume of air you take in.

- ❋ Your next few breaths will probably be deeper, like a series of involuntary sighs of relief. It is what's called *prana* in Sanskrit and *pneuma* in Greek—the impression that the universe is breathing through you.

- ❋ As you draw your fifth or sixth breath, your mind begins to wander. Don't worry. Let the formlessness of your thoughts fill the emptiness in your chest.

- ❋ Don't expect to be blissfully self-aware by the time you take your seventh or eighth breath. Like breathing, consciousness is an in-and-out process. We inhale and exhale. In the same way we remember and forget.

Be inspired—one breath at a time.

the art of meditating

To achieve a state of higher consciousness—to be what is called *mindful*—you must empty your mind. But how can a mind be both empty and full? This is just one of the many contradictions that have kept meditation experts arguing back and forth for centuries. Quiet your mind, they admonish. Don't wait for the other shoe to drop. Consciousness is not a state of doing but a state of being.

"You must seek without seeking," say the Zen masters. The trick, they explain, is to be here, now. Sit still, clear your mind, wait. The built-in suspense will keep you awake.

The word *meditation* has the same root as the word *medicine*. The first thing you notice when you start to meditate is how good it makes you feel. Most mind-silencing techniques require you to relax, close your eyes, and focus on internal imagery—all rather pleasant things. During the first few seconds, you experience a healing sensation. Harmless and effective, meditation could very well be an over-the-counter drug.

Unfortunately, the stuff is volatile—you can't bottle it.

Few people can maintain a calm composure for more than a couple of minutes. As soon as you think you have achieved some sort of mental balance, you congratulate yourself. The next thing you know, you are chasing your thoughts up some tree.

The meditation exercises championed by all spiritual teachers, from traditional masters to self-styled gurus, are never the cure-alls they promise to be. They are too exacting for an average person with a minor-league attention span. In all likelihood, only a handful of disciples can really practice what their teachers preach.

If you ever tried the Tao of Breathing, or attempted to visualize the Tibetan Wheel of Life, or struggled to attain the Hasidic ideal of continual remembrance of God, you know what I mean.

After a couple of minutes, you lose your concentration and begin to fudge a step or two. It's only human, after all. But instead of admitting that you are daydreaming, you subconsciously embellish your practice and imagine that you are achieving lofty results.

Could it be that meditation techniques are in fact designed to test our intellectual honesty more than our spiritual abilities?

"Sit quietly, doing nothing," instructs the Zen master.
"Spring comes and the grass grows of itself."

Paradoxically, it is when we accept that we can't meditate that meditation starts to work. Instead of being a success-oriented venture, the practice becomes a humble reminder of how difficult it is for any of us to stay in touch with ordinary reality.

Forewarned is forearmed. Meditation baits us with a promise of inner peace and serenity, but as soon as we are hooked, we find ourselves flopping around, with nothing to hold on to but our meditation pillows, our mantras, and our punctured egos.

In that vulnerable state, we are ready to be enlightened.

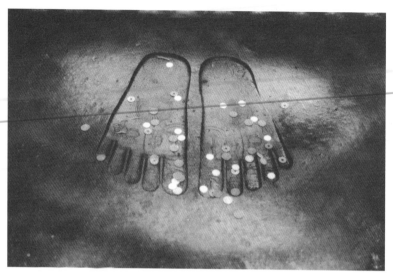

To be enlightened is to know oneself—and not run away.

WHAT IS ENLIGHTENMENT?

It can take a few weeks, a few months, a few years—or, according to some religions, a few lifetimes—before you begin to understand what's called *satori* in Japanese, *wu-wei* in Chinese, *samadhi* in Tibetan, *d'vekut* in Hebrew, and conversion in Christian lore—before you become a candidate for enlightenment.

Zen Buddhists, enlightenment specialists par excellence, define the phenomenon as a sudden spiritual enhancement, one that triggers an abrupt shift in viewpoint. Hundreds of Zen stories tell of how monks failed to attain *satori* after decades of practice, only to stumble on it as if by accident. These anecdotes are interpreted as evidence that you can only prepare for spiritual change, you cannot control it.

Reaching enlightenment is a bit like winning the lottery—not a million-dollar bonanza, mind you, just fifty bucks. The odds are in your favor. Years later, you'll laugh remembering how sudden yet how anticlimatic the event really was. You'll wonder why it wasn't more emotional or dramatic.

You probably weren't meditating. Chances are you were waiting for the light to change at an intersection, or looking out the window while talking on the phone, or washing the dishes after a party. It hit you without warning. You were not prepared for it. No one can expect the unexpected—no one is ever ready to be enlightened.

Your moment of enlightenment came packaged as a thought bubble. On a scale of one to ten, it was probably a number four insight.

Maybe you realized that no matter what, you will always be able to pay the rent.

Or you stopped feeling as if it was your God-given duty to be right all the time.

Or you saw the blue veins in your hands as if for the first time.

It changed your life.

Enlightenment is just another word for feeling comfortable with being a completely ordinary person.

At long last, the unexceptional seems extraordinary enough: a puddle of water, a child running after a bird, the peaceful hum of your computer—and you, in the midst of it all, with your unvarnished self-image.

The charade is over and a painful existential headache is gone. You are not a perfect being—far from it—but your mind is clear. For the first time perhaps, you feel unflustered, alert, and ready to go.

Cats know everything there is to know about meditation.

Be Still—Not Stiff

Think of meditation as an attempt to tame this wild and furtive creature we sometimes call the soul. Like an undomesticated animal that's easily spooked by noise, your high-strung virtual self goes scampering away as soon as there is static in the air. Before you can come near this shy *anima*—your inner stray cat, so to speak—learn to tread lightly. Approach meditation as mindfully as a feline exploring new territory.

- Either sitting in a chair or standing, alternately press the toes of your right foot and left foot lightly on the floor to establish contact with the ground.
- Mentally draw a line that connects the top of your head with your right toes.
- Draw another line that connects the top of your head with your left toes.
- Imagine that these lines are rubber bands. Stretch them a bit. Test their resiliency.
- Keep tugging at these head-to-toes tethers. Don't lose your elastic connection to the floor—or to your head.
- Now you can sit quietly. But don't let your body slacken or go stiff. Put a bounce in your seat.
- Don't try to entrap your mind. Harness it with the stretchy rubber bridle of your attention.

4

the art of lounging

t the end of the day, it is critical you take your mind off things and let your thoughts idle for a while. Regardless of how tired you are, give your cognitive self a chance to come home before you go to sleep. Bring your attention back down to earth, literally.

Find a low chair—a couple of pillows, a footstool, or a tree stump will also do—and drop down by about

34

three feet, so that your eyes are where your navel was when you were standing. What happens next is called lounging. It requires that you stay put for a while and wait for your head to return to its senses. Don't move until your brain is safely back in its skull.

Lounging in the evening is a private endeavor, even if you are among family and friends; it's one of the few communal activities that allows you to be alone if you choose to be—and no one will accuse you of being a loner.

You can sit on the porch by yourself, swaying back and forth on the old swing while relatives chat a few feet away.

You can meet acquaintances at a bar for happy hour, but instead of talking, let the hubbub of the place wash over you like the sound of the surf.

Or, after the kids are in bed, you can sink into your favorite chair and savor the silence of the night.

Lounging takes patience, so settle down comfortably in an easy chair. Ironically, though, easy chairs are everything but easy: They are carefully engineered to make it difficult for you to scramble to your feet.

Try to get up? The angle of the seat sucks you right back in.

Grab the armrests? They yield when you tug at them.

Bend forward to extract yourself from the embrace of pillows? Your head is no counterweight for your hindquarters.

The pelvic girdle is the heaviest bone structure in the body—far heftier than the cranial cavity. Once it is resting on a low ledge, you might as well have dropped an anchor.

Which is exactly what's needed to prevent your thoughts from bobbing around.

Most important, lounging coaxes you into changing your point of view. Instead of maneuvering in a layer of reality that's five to six feet above ground, you are now dealing

The perfect way to spend an afternoon in Provence.

with an underworld that's only three feet from your toes.

You get to see the room from a new angle and observe things that are usually hidden: the insides of lamp shades, the spines of old books relegated to bottom shelves, flower stems wilting in vases, paint peeling on windowsills.

Before you know it, you find yourself staring at a brass handle on a drawer, marveling at its craftsmanship. Curious as a cat, your mind joins you in this investigation. It counts the screws that hold the handle in place. Only three! One is missing. You are tempted to get up and see if you have a replacement screw in your toolbox—but the

Like water eroding stone, idle contemplation erodes tensions.

damned chair keeps you pinned down. So you sink a little deeper and resume your silent contemplation.

WEAR DOWN YOUR RESTLESSNESS

Quieting down mental activity isn't easy. You've managed to pull your mind back to earth. Now comes the hard part. If you sit tight, you have an opportunity to let your ideas, conjectures, and observations sort themselves out all on their own.

Some of the best thinking we do happens when the conscious mind is on a sabbatical.

Isaac Newton figured out the law of universal gravitation when sitting under a tree.

Ben Franklin invented the lightning rod while flying a kite.

Thomas Edison came up with the light-bulb filament while idly rolling kerosene residue between his fingers.

Albert Einstein pondered the riddle of the universe with a cat on his lap.

So don't get up yet. Contribute to science. Stay prone as long as you can.

To resist the temptation of getting up, shift to geological time. Reclining as you are, with your center of gravity close to the floor, you might as well be a mountain range—your body a succession of peaks and valleys, your feet two promontories at the end of a peninsula.

Let your thoughts go back and forth over the odds and ends of the day. Don't be afraid to wear down what's on the surface of ordinary life in order to expose the rock bottom of your feelings.

Erosion is a slow process, but it's a creative one. It's how the earth chisels mountains, carves canyons, makes sand dunes, and subdivides continents.

Tips for Beach Bums

We love to stretch out on the beach because the sun makes us feel drowsy. But beware, some dermatologists contend that this torpid, mind-numbed sensation is nothing more than an allergic reaction to the sun's harmful ultraviolet rays. Protect your health and save your skin by getting out of the harsh midday sun. There are ways to enjoy the beach (and quiet the mind) that do not require you to put your life on the line.

- Wear a straw hat:

    The world looks serene beyond the brim of a Panama.

- Mold your body into the hot sand:

    Experience the fluidity of the ground.

- Walk into the surf with a shirt on:

    Imagine that you are an exotic jellyfish.

- Feel the salt on your lips:

    Iodine promotes mental alertness.

- Look at infinity:

    Let your thoughts conform with the horizon.

Emulate wise sunbathers who always keep their shirts on.

the art of yawning

A sudden internal event that stretches muscles from the inside out, yawning is an invigorating form of exercise for people who are naturally—and unapologetically—lazy. As a fitness routine, it's actually quite effective. You overachievers out there, give it a try.

The yawn feels at first like a tiny vortex of low pressure somewhere in the middle of the head. Soon it

spreads through the entire body in a spiraling, twisterlike motion: It dilates your pharynx, larynx, nostrils, and bronchial tubes; it lifts your eyebrows and your shoulders; it lowers your diaphragm to let your lungs expand; it makes your heart race and increases the flow of blood to your brain. Then, in a dramatic gyration, it returns to your head, where it gets your tongue to retreat and forces your mandibles to move sideways and down.

All this happens in less than six seconds. When it's over, you feel a little wobbly perhaps—but a lot more limber.

The commonly held belief is that yawning is the body's response to an excess of carbon dioxide in the blood. When yawning, we send a blast of oxygen to the brain. But some neuroscientists disagree. Subjects who were given whiffs of oxygen still yawned.

A mysterious reflex, yawning seems to be connected with health: People who are acutely ill or severely psychotic hardly ever feel the need to wrench their faces open.

The dictionary tells us that the yawn is an involuntary response to fatigue and boredom. If this is true, then nature spares no expense to shake our doldrums and make sure there is never a dull moment.

So, when weariness builds up like a sluggish weather system inside your head, go ahead and yawn to your heart's content. Open your mouth as wide as possible and unhinge your jaw. It releases an invisible funnel of pent-up energy that travels through your body, clearing partially blocked tunnels and chimneys—the auditory tubes, the lachrymal-nasal passages, and the lymphatic ducts, as well as larger vents like the trachea and the lungs. You can feel your ears pop as the pressure equalizes between this internal labyrinth of intersecting corridors and the outside world.

Yawning is a total-body stretch, something like yoga but without the contorted

Yawn—and catch a glimpse of the infinite emptiness surrounding you.

postures and the breathing exercises, without the torso and leg twists and the stomach-sucking techniques.

Yawning is so pleasantly effortless, it is contagious—another scientific riddle. Few people can resist the sight of someone drop-ping their jaw without immediately being compelled to do the same. The mere mention of the word *yawning* in a conversation is sometimes enough to make your nose twitch, your eyes water, and the inside of your mouth stretch like a rubber band.

One explanation for this phenomenon could be that we are all interconnected after all. It is almost as if the human race were a huge ventilation system for souls: Create a draft at one end of the system by opening your mouth wide, and soon, around you, everyone's jaws, nostrils, and eardrums begin to bang and rap like so many loose doors and unlatched windows. Yawning in public is not advisable—you could start a chain reaction of awesome proportions.

NATURAL REFLEXOLOGY

To get over a yawn, you must open a hatch somewhere. But if politeness prevails and you can't release this internal pressure through the air, you have another option: Drive it through the ground.

Think of your body as a lightning rod of sorts. Through your feet, you can channel excess energy into the earth. You've probably noticed that the first thing most of us do when we get home is kick off our shoes. With that gesture, we reestablish direct contact with the ground. Through the soles of our feet we release painful tensions.

In social situations, grounding can be a little more difficult. In restaurants, women discreetly remove their high heels under the table and allow their toes to furl and unfurl while the waiter enumerates the specials on the menu. Men extend their legs in front of them (making sure they don't inadvertently crush some discarded pairs of heels), stretch their Achilles tendons, and grind their heels into the ground.

Reflexology, an ancient Chinese healing technique, is based on the same grounding principles. Practitioners of this form of alternative medicine help restore the flow of energy throughout the body by massaging

The sky starts right under your feet.

specific points on the feet. Press here and you can lessen lower-back pain; press there and you can ease stomach problems or flush away headaches. Usually, after a few minutes of expert foot massaging, you are so relaxed you fall asleep.

Wiggling toes—the poor man's reflexology—is just as effective. Try the following:

Spread out your toes, hold them in this stretched position for ten seconds, and release. Repeat the procedure three or four times. Notice how it affects the upper part of your body: how, without further ado, your sinuses seem to clear, your breathing becomes more even, your forehead relaxes, and your ears—like your toes—tingle with pleasure.

Of course, if you are in polite society, none of these shenanigans will do. When the conversation gets boring and you feel like you might yawn, all you can pray for is a chance to shift your weight from right to left while pretending to listen. If things get really dull, sway back and forth imperceptibly. In a pinch, always remember that you can maintain a state of internal buoyancy by pushing gently against the floor with different parts of your feet: heels, arches, big toes, digits. Keep a live connection with the ground and you'll drive away fatigue, boredom, tension—and the urge to expose your teeth in public.

Stretch Your Imagination

Fight the ho-hums by playing tricks on your mind. The following "brain games" are inspired by Japanese koans, those mental puzzles designed to help Zen students let go of their basic assumptions about the rational world.

- Scramble time: It's Monday afternoon? Make believe it's Friday P.M.— just for a few minutes.

- Change your destiny: In your favorite magazine, read someone else's horoscope as if it were your own.

- Challenge the written word: Visualize the word *red* in bright blue letters; spell out the word *river* and see a pebble in your mind's eye; write *lips,* but imagine a cloud.

- Fight illiteracy: Learn to say "I don't know." Not knowing is the opposite of ignorance. Each time you say "I don't know," your curiosity grows—and the universe expands.

- Question patriarchy: Casually ask both partners in a couple if they would ever consider taking their spouse's paternal grandmother's maiden name as their own. Then sit back and listen.

- Practice compassion: Never forget that for everyone on earth, there was once a pregnant woman who couldn't see her body past her belly button.

Experience "being" rather than "doing." Give yourself permission to be bored.

the art of napping

f you've got too much to do, take a nap—just a ten-minute nap. As ludicrous as it seems, dropping off the edge of consciousness is often the best way to steal the extra time you need to meet crushing deadlines.

Burrowing under a light blanket of sleep in the middle of a busy day is not unlike digging an escape tunnel—one that bypasses impossible work schedules,

Consider the lilies of the field. . . . They toil not, neither do they spin.

conflicting agendas, and programming headaches—and lets you resurface minutes later with a fresh outlook on life.

John F. Kennedy, Winston Churchill, Thomas Edison, Napoleon Bonaparte, and Leonardo da Vinci practiced the art of mid-

day shut-eye. Like them, you may discover that dozing behind people's backs gives you the advantage.

Sleep research shows that below the surface of a peaceful snooze, a complex physiological process is taking place. What looks from the outside like inertia is, in fact, an active internal state teeming with rapidly firing neurons.

While we sleep, sophisticated sequences of brain waves transform our inert bodies into humming power stations that produce intelligence, alertness, and discernment.

There is overwhelming scientific evidence that lack of sleep brings about a severe deterioration of consciousness: fatigue, inability to concentrate, visual and tactile hallucinations.

The urge to curl up in the early afternoon is a warning signal that you are running low on common sense and good judgment. This is the time of day when the number of traffic and industrial accidents rises—when people fall asleep at the wheel or the switch.

It is far better to conk out than trigger a disaster. Flat on your back, you can enter a manufacturing mode as you fabricate the building blocks of your next waking state.

Surrendering to slumber does more than just restore the ability to function efficiently—it actually generates that clear and transparent state of mind we call wakefulness.

DEALING WITH
A GUILTY
CONSCIENCE

Wide awake, the conscious mind is unnerved by the idea that sofa sleeping could be construed as an active endeavor.

To make sure you don't dillydally among pillows when you should be doing spreadsheets, your guilty conscience has you convinced that logging Z's with your clothes on is a crime against capitalism.

What do you expect? The cognitive self cannot comprehend its own noncognitive genesis. Rather than let you enjoy a harmless snooze, your conscience compels you to plod all afternoon through the leaden and airless biosphere of the doze-deprived.

Don't waste any time explaining to your superego that ten minutes in sweet limbo won't compromise your fifteen minutes of fame. In a land inhabited by insomniacs, nappers will always be under suspicion.

In Latin countries, it's the opposite. People who don't nap are considered odd. In Italy, Spain, and the South of France, the siesta is a sacred, postlunch, digestive ritual observed by all, except tourists.

Like Noël Coward's proverbial mad dogs and Englishmen, non-natives wander around, oblivious of the harsh midday sun, while the locals wisely retire for forty-five minutes in the shade. Banks, museums, post offices, churches, and shops lock their doors. The traffic ebbs as torpor engulfs the city. In the privacy of their bedrooms, citizens relax behind closed shutters.

The best you can do on this side of the Atlantic is let your internal monitor default to the screen-saver mode, rub your eyes, and lean back.

Or close the door, lie down under your desk, and rest your head on an accordion file.

More entrepreneurial nappers find a couch in an empty office.

Power snoozers catch up on their beauty sleep ensconced in their wing chairs.

Young mothers lullaby their babies in rocking slumber.

The brown-bag lunchtime crowd compensates for its late-night TV habit on scruffy patches of urban grass.

Road warriors sneak out to the parking lot, slip into their cars, put their driver's seats in the full recline position, and go to sleep with their stocking feet up on their steering wheels.

Just before you pass out, admit it: A touch of guilt adds to the forbidden allure of daytime Z's.

Recipe for a Gourmet Nap

The long afternoon nap is for sleep connoisseurs—it's an after-dessert delicacy.
To make sure you wake up refreshed, follow these easy steps.

1. If you don't have shutters, draw the blinds or the curtains. The room should be bathed in a soft, restful glow.

2. Kick off your shoes. Only remove garments that are constricting or that would rumple badly. You want to be somewhat dressed up for the occasion: The gourmet nap is a formal affair.

3. Glance at the clock, take off your watch, and decide when you want to wake up. Trust your subconscious to nudge you when your time is up.

4. Lie down under the covers but *not* between the sheets.

5. Close your eyes and imagine that you are in a small boat, about to embark on a short journey. Pull up the anchor and let the boat drift. The water may feel choppy at first, but soon the waves will diminish and you'll be sailing on a smooth sea.

6. You'll be awakened by a bump—your keel is scraping a sandy bottom. Drag yourself out of bed slowly, as if you were pulling your skiff onto a beach.

7. Throw water on your face, stretch, open the window. Don't rush. You've got plenty of time ahead of you.

the art of bathing

Y ou don't have to take a bath to be in a bath. Even out of water, we are soaking in the warm aquarium of our own cells. Two-thirds of the weight of the human body is from a liquid that has roughly the same density and chemical composition as the salty broth of the sea.

When our ancestors crawled out of the ocean to become land creatures, they took with them reserves of

water large enough to survive an evolutionary drought. To take a bath, then, is to return briefly to our original aquatic state.

We have more in common with dolphins than with apes. A streamlined layer of fat under our hairless skin gives us the buoyancy of a sea mammal. Our upright position allows us to keep our heads above water. Breath control enables us to dive, but also to whistle and chirp like our bottle-nosed friends.

The liquid environment, it seems, restores our natural ability to play with sounds. People who are otherwise shy and self-conscious sing or vocalize in the bathtub. Psychiatrists have noticed that patients who can't communicate on dry land are more likely to pipe up once they are immersed in a tub. Children take to water with shrieks of delight. And one wonders if, inside the womb, unborn babies squeal like tiny sea otters when they paddle around in the sub-tropical water of their amniotic caves.

Less strenuous than land exercises, water workouts use less oxygen, making it available to the brain. This could be why premature babies fare better when nurtured back to health in a warm-water environment.

In Russia, mothers are sometimes encouraged to give birth in warm pools: "Water babies," as their newborns are called, enter the world wide-eyed and peaceful, and cry only when they are brought to the surface.

Skinny-dipping at home in the privacy of your bathroom lets you connect with your primordial marine self, but it also lets you journey downstream into the hydrosphere—into the 330,000,000 cubic miles of water that circulate on or near the surface of the Earth.

In the big watery scheme of things, your plumbing is as much a part of nature as is dew on a spiderweb or a storm gathering over Miami.

To penetrate into this ever-flowing liquid domain, just submerge your ears below the surface and listen to the sloshing of the invisible underworld: the gurgling in your stomach, the pulsing in your throat, the swishing of the bathwater—but also the gushing sound of a distant drain, the sudden deluge of a neighbor's toilet, and the muffled rumble of hundreds of pipes, conduits, sewers, and gutters that prevent human installations from turning into swamps.

Like a huge enameled seashell, your bathtub is a listening device that lets you eavesdrop on the constant percolation of water in the universe.

All ears to the murmur of this subterranean hydro-system, you soon become blissfully unaware of the drops of sweat on your brow, the steam in the air, and the condensation on the ceiling. No longer concerned about where your body ends and where the hydrosphere begins, you sink deeper into the tub. Imperceptibly, you drift toward the drain. If someone were to pull the plug right now, you probably would offer no resistance and happily go out with the bathwater! After a twenty-minute soak, you wouldn't care—you would be one with the flow.

WHAT'S HYDROTHERAPY?

The most popular form of bathing is hydrotherapy—simply soaking in warm or cool water. The technique capitalizes on the physical and mechanical properties of water to promote mental health and relaxation.

Submerged in water, you have the impression of being a lot lighter than you are on land (you may feel as if you've lost one hundred pounds or more when you float at the deep end of a swimming pool).

In Japan, hydrotherapy is believed to restore health—
and dissolve sin.

Unlike land gravity, which pulls you downward, water presses on you in all directions, giving you a gentle head-to-toe body tuck. The bigger the tub or the deeper the pool, the more lithe you become. Gone are the bloated feeling, the backache, the joint pain, the sore muscles. The even resistance of H_2O molecules against your skin tones your silhouette better than reinforced, control-top Lycra underwear.

In ancient cultures, hydrotherapy had spiritual overtones. For the Romans, for instance, cleanliness was next to godliness—it was a citizen's moral duty to patronize public baths.

In Japan, for centuries people have stood under sacred waterfalls to try to calm their minds.

In India, along the Ganges, pilgrims by the thousands immerse themselves in the sluggish stream of the holy river.

In the Judeo-Christian tradition, baptism is still a rite of passage, a dunking ritual not unlike rebirthing.

WHAT'S
AROMATHERAPY?

Aromatherapy is olfactory-enhanced hydrotherapy. By mixing scented essential oils into a bath, you add a stimulating component to the soothing qualities of warm water. This technique is believed to have a rejuvenating effect on your health—and on your memory.

The evocative power of long-forgotten fragrances from childhood can bring back a heightened sense of well-being, the likes of which you have not experienced since your baby-faced, downy-cheeked days.

But aromatherapy isn't just about the sweet smell of eucalyptus, bergamot, or chamomile. Reminiscent of our grandmoth-

Ancient spa ritual in Jaipur: Pilgrims gather at a sacred village pool.

ers' smelling salts, pungent and unexpected scents are sometimes used to invigorate the senses and stimulate body functions.

Added to bathwater, a surprisingly pleasant mixture of turpentine and milk, for instance, is gaining popularity in Europe for its healing effect on the respiratory and digestive systems.

In this country, health spas blend their own bath oils, reaching into the psyches of their guests with subtle fragrances that release primordial memories. Under a veil of lavender and rosemary, let's say, you may detect the faint odor of instant lemonade combined with just a whiff of mosquito repellent. These odd trace elements will conjure up images from that first backpacking trip in Vermont—and turn your bathing experience into a soothing nostalgia immersion.

HOW ABOUT BALNEOTHERAPY?

Balneotherapy is the third, and the most controversial, of all bathing techniques. It's an old-world healing tradition that takes advantage of the chemical or mineral content of natural hot springs or deep seawater. Water cures, as the balneo treatments are often called, go beyond simple bathing.

The various therapies include a wide range of exotic procedures such as thalassotherapy (showers and soaking rituals using marine products), full-body wraps (more like embalming than bathing), herbal soaks (you feel like a tea bag), steam treatments, and dips in volcanic-looking mud pits.

Unlike aromatherapy, which smells good, balneotherapy often smells foul. Natural sulfur, microscopic algae, or live enzymes in the water can test your olfactory sensibility. But regular visitors to the great spas of Europe, where balneotherapy is still very popular, swear by it.

Here and abroad, you can find commercial—and deodorized—versions of balneo products. These natural ointments, balms, liniments, tonics, and poultices are usually available at spa gift shops and in health-food stores, ready for you to try at home. Go ahead, it's not dangerous. But plan to take an honest-to-goodness, no-gimmicks, hydrotherapy bath when your balneo treatment is over.

If there is water, there is life.

A Forgotten Home Remedy

Before the invention of antibiotics, people in Europe cured their colds by dunking their arms in hot water. It induced a short-term high fever and was believed to rid the body of toxins.

- Pull a chair in front of your wash basin and stack a couple of pillows on the seat so that you can sit comfortably in front of the sink, as if you were at your desk.
- Get into your pajamas, tie your hair up, and roll up your sleeves. Check the clock. The procedure should last no more than twenty minutes.
- Fill the basin with hot water. Add scented bath oils if you wish.
- Cover your head and face with a fresh towel.
- Cross your bare arms in front of you and submerge them.
- Every five minutes, raise the temperature of the bath by reaching out and adding hot water right from the tap.
- The steam releases sweat from every pore of your skin. You are a rosy—and drippy—mess.
- Your twenty minutes are over. Get up, dry your arms and your face, and go straight to bed. You should sleep like a baby and wake up full of energy.

the art of tasting

I n its buoyant perfection, the chocolate mousse lures your spoon as surely as the candle lures the moth. The only way to satisfy your curiosity is to dip in. Under the dark velvety surface, a mysterious world of impressions beckons you.

We eat to nourish our bodies, but we taste food to satiate our minds. No dainty eater, the brain feasts on the aroma and flavor of each bite we bring to our lips

Fresh produce is food for thought.

long before the stomach has a chance to get a piece of the action. It only takes one-tenth of a second for nose and tongue to round up every wafting molecule in food—from whiffs of aromatic phenol to hints of mouth-watering ethyl acetate—and deliver them to our hungry neurons.

Digesting the taste of food requires great mental concentration. In the twinkling of an eye, our cortex absorbs the data provided by more than five million smell- and taste-sensing cells—and combines it with the color, shape, temperature, texture, and sound of the food ingested. Stored forever in our memory banks, this bundle of serendipitous sensations is what scientists call *flavor.*

Unusual or exotic dishes can cause gluttons and gourmets alike to close their eyes and feel momentarily light-headed—so intense and sudden is the rush created by the mental activity required to decipher complex tastes. To get a sense of how much information is packed in the flavor of food, consider the work of Marcel Proust. With just one tiny bite into a madeleine cake, the French writer unexpectedly retrieved enough material from his memory to write *Remembrance of Things Past,* a twelve-volume, stream-of-consciousness masterpiece—and one of the longest novels in modern literature.

People who eat slowly are usually more involved with their minds than their bellies. Tasting food is one of the most pleasant ways to stimulate your thoughts. Next time you sit in front of a great meal, take a minute to explore the texture of the food—its hardness, brittleness, chewiness, and viscosity—as well as its color, resiliency, and even sound. Let the fragility of a ginger snap or the satiny finish of a creamed sauce suggest a memory or a word to you.

When tasting a wine, brood over the visual and olfactory particularities of the liquid before drinking it. It is almost with reluctance that enologists bring a glass to their lips. Their taste buds, they know, will only confirm the elaborate impressions they have already gathered through careful observation.

Like wine tasting, tea tasting is a lengthy procedure that involves scrutinizing the color of dry leaves versus that of infused ones, and comparing their respective smells at various temperatures.

When tasting tea, experts suck the liquid in order to make as much noise as possible. Legend has it that, just by listening to the sound of tea percolating between their teeth, astute Indian tea-tasters can tell whether the water used for a particular brew came from a well, reservoir, or spring.

In Japan, the tea ceremony is choreographed to give guests a chance to indulge in poetic reverie and share the expression of their wisdom with other participants. The serene decor of the tearoom incites them to marvel at the effortless elegance of the flower arrangement, at the sobriety of the lines of the painted scroll on the wall, and at the lovely simplicity of the teacups. While sipping green tea, they taste the flavor of their most insightful thoughts.

WHAT'S ON THE TIP OF YOUR TONGUE?

Butterflies carry most of their taste buds on their front legs: They can evaluate the sweetness of a flower simply by landing on it. Some types of fish sport their gustatory organs on their fins, others on their tails: They savor the water as they swim. We taste our food with the tongue, the same organ we use to speak: Not surprisingly, we have a natural propensity to talk with our mouths full.

Eventually, we learn to clear our palates before wagging our tongues. But rich and scrumptious food always invites us to voice our satisfaction aloud. Stimulated taste buds can turn the most taciturn among us into poets. Hosts measure the success of a meal by the number and the originality of the adjectives that come to their guests' lips as they taste a dish.

The development of gourmet food is closely associated with refinements in the art of conversation. The French, those accomplished gourmands, are never at a loss for words. In this country, where repartee is not always on the menu, we judge a restaurant by the decibel level in the room. If the place is too quiet when we walk in, we are tempted to turn around and leave. If, on the contrary, the ambience is boisterous and noisy, we assume that the food will be delicious. Reinforcing this perception are rambling waiters who try to whet the appetite of patrons with long-winded recipe descriptions.

As far as the cook is concerned, vocabulary is destiny—the vocabulary of the dinner guests, that is. Conversationally challenged gourmands are not as much fun to entertain as gossiping friends, chattering revelers, amusing keynote speakers, or folks who never tire of proposing toasts.

Unfortunately, adjectives that do justice to gastronomical excellence are in short supply in the universe. The average person uses the same two or three expressions over and over to show gustatory appreciation—words like *scrumptious, delicious, delectable*—a meager showing compared with the extensive jargon most of us use to show disapproval. Chefs would do well to cook up a new mouthwatering lexicon to describe their culinary treats. "Flavorsome" and "finger-lickin' good" are just no match for some of the succulent offerings of contemporary cuisine.

Our physiological makeup explains this linguistic shortcoming. In human beings, taste

You will forget the taste— but never the flavor.

buds are much more sensitive to bitter, salty, and sour substances than they are to sweet

In France, the greatest compliment to the chef
is good conversation.

food. The sides and back of the tongue, as well as the soft palate, feature taste buds that specialize in recognizing acidity, sharpness, pungency, rancidity, acerbity, and tartness. Buried inside papillae and strategically positioned wherever they can catch the most food, our taste buds are part of the body's early-warning system. In the back, near the entrance to the throat, they stand by, ready to make us gag rather than let poisonous substances slip down our throats.

The tip of the tongue is the only region of the mouth that clearly registers the presence of sugar. This tiny gustatory domain tracks down sweet-tasting high-energy food—the kind that revs up the activity in the brain, which is why it is such a sweet sensation to discover the right word poised on the tip of your tongue.

How to Drink and Stay Sober

Learn to hold your liquor—literally. How you hold a glass of wine can make the difference between staying sober and getting buzzed. Borrow a couple of tricks from wine-tasting pros and you'll never have to call a cab to go home and apologize to your host the next day.

- Always raise your glass in front of your eyes before you begin to drink. Sit straight, breathe easy, and make a silent toast to Bacchus, god of inebriety—your adversary for the evening.
- Don't cling to your glass. Keep a respectful distance. When you are not drinking, the edge of your glass should be at least eight inches from the tip of your nose.
- Never look up at the ceiling when you drink. Look through the glass, straight into the room.
- Every so often, bring the glass to your lips, tilt it, inhale the aroma—but don't drink.
- Don't ever take a mindless swig. Taste the wine as you swallow. The secret to remaining sober is to appreciate what you drink.

the art of listening

ur ears crave sound bites. Word-of-mouth is a dish we find irresistible. Attracted by the prospect of some juicy, firsthand scoop, few of us can let the phone ring, ignore office gossip, or turn off the TV just before the evening news. The sound of the human voice triggers in all of us a delicious sense of anticipation and urgency.

Our auditory systems are ultrasensitive acoustical

instruments that can identify, perceive, and decode speech—whether we are whispering in the dark or screaming over the din of the noisiest restaurant.

Even in the worst listening conditions, our brains can reconstruct words and get the gist of what is being said. Our cognitive functions are trained to lift isolated clues—sounds, lip movements, intonations, pauses, stammers, smiles, smirks, and frowns—and patch them together into an apparently seamless verbal expression.

Our cortices are wired to finish other people's sentences.

A major portion of what we think we just heard is the product of our imaginations. Without even knowing it, we fill missing gaps in other people's utterances, correcting their grammar, interpreting their accents, adding punctuation, substituting words—all in all, creating *their* speech as they go along.

Usually, we can figure out what people are trying to say long before they stop rambling. Far from being passive, listening to someone talk is an active, inspired, and often compassionate act of creation.

Phonemic restoration, as this process is called, is a useful survival skill—a critical asset if you are trying to hear what the skipper is saying over the howling of a storm or if, James Bond–style, you are deciphering voice messages transmitted through a microchip in your wristwatch.

In normal conditions, though—in the boardroom, the classroom, the living room, or the bedroom—phonemic restoration can create communication snafus. Before you struggle to sort out what he said she said, and what she said he said, remember that there are no clear boundaries between speaking and listening.

The next time you attend a meeting, sit back, relax, listen. Be the designated listener. Note how much concentration it takes just to follow every word of a verbal exchange.

Listening to nothing is more intriguing than listening for something.

You don't have to talk to be an active participant: As far as others are concerned, every one of your glances, head movements, smiles, or facial expressions is part of what is being said.

The more you listen to others, the more they will seek your approval. Vigilance is a powerful magnet. When focused, your attention acts as the baton of a conductor. Silently, you can orchestrate the flow of ideas, influence the outcome of the conversation—or add to the confusion. Whoever listens most usually controls the situation.

L I S T E N   T O   Y O U R
I N T U I T I O N

In a quiet environment, our brains can process five hundred spoken words per minute. Unfortunately, even the most eloquent orators can't satisfy our ravenous appetites for auditory stimulation.

Most speakers deliver an average of only one hundred fifty words per minute—and that's assuming they express themselves in complete sentences. After a while, this three-hundred-fifty-word lag time can tax the patience of any audience.

The most alert among us use this reprieve to listen to their intuition. They engage their eyes as much as their ears. Good listeners are also attentive spectators. While following a discussion, they scrutinize the facial expressions, haircut, jewelry, clothes, and body language of the person talking.

When the presentation is over, you should be able to describe accurately the look of the speaker and the quality of his or her voice. But don't expect to be able to repeat what was said. Too few and far apart, the words themselves probably left only a vague impression.

Maybe it's just as well. Stop beating up your brain if you draw a blank when trying to remember the details of a conversation. According to a major university study, intellectual content accounts for only 7 percent of all verbal communication.

What passes between a speaker and a listener goes way beyond the mere sharing of words.

We feel vibrations in speech, even though we can't always hear them. Whereas some tones trigger auditory responses, others affect our moods or provoke unexpected trains of thought.

It's all legitimate information.

For instance, a friend calls on the phone, allegedly to seek your advice. After listening for less than a minute, you know in your bones that all she really wants to do is talk.

Or a client congratulates you on a job well done. Your gut warns you that in the next breath he will begin to make excuses for not paying you the full amount.

Over lunch, your mother tells you that everything is fine—dandy, in fact—and instantly your stomach goes into a knot.

When people speak, they produce audible as well as inaudible vibrations. What we don't pick up with our ears, we register with other parts of our anatomy: our bone structure, our heartbeat, the liquid content of our intercellular structure. To listen well is to

When we share secrets, we share more than words.

turn your body into a sounding board for other people's thoughts, ideas, and emotions.

When Silence Is Golden

So, you are an expert on German typography, Japanese puppetry, or French cuisine? Don't bring the subject up in public. The English describe a gentleman as someone who can play the bagpipes—but doesn't.

- Not talking about your favorite subject will keep it that way.
- Not getting recognition will ensure you don't become complacent.
- Not strutting your stuff in front of new acquaintances will endear you to your old friends.
- Not letting the world in on your secret passion will add to your mystery.
- Not bragging will ward off envy.
- Not tooting your horn will save you from becoming a bore.
- Not saying anything when you have nothing to say will always prove wise.
- Not asking for the answer will give you time to ponder the question.

Leave something unsaid. Don't give every detail. Make room for mystery.

the art of waiting

In the pursuit of tomorrow, we often run into scheduling potholes—those waiting periods that force us to linger in the present tense. Stuck in the "now" (for how long, we don't know), we must wait patiently for the next available ride into the future. It is a chance to take a breather. But no. Far from enjoying the lull, we feel frustrated, impatient, jittery. We look at our watches and are annoyed to find them still

ticking. One of our worst fears is to be left behind as the world rushes toward its destiny.

We firmly believe that time flows in a continuous stream, twenty-four hours a day, rain or shine. But, so far, no scientist or philosopher has been able to prove without a doubt that time goes in one direction, from left to right, from the past into the future.

Sure, time can be measured, but it can be plotted only in relation to a number of other phenomena, like the position of the sun or the ticking of the energy inside atoms. In and of itself, time doesn't seem to exist.

No wonder we feel foolish when we are made to wait: We are trapped in an invisible cobweb of our own making.

As far as time researchers are concerned, only one thing is sure: Watched pots never boil. Various studies have shown that when people are forced to wait, seconds seem to go at a snail's pace, a speed equivalent to seventy minutes per hour.

On the other hand, time flies when you're having fun. Experiments prove that our perception of time shrinks dramatically when the waiting period is punctuated with a series of brief stimuli—either auditory or visual—delivered at regular intervals.

We experience waiting as dead space between two beats. The faster the rhythm, the less we tarry. Time don't mean a thing if it ain't got that swing.

When waiting for someone who is late, don't scrutinize the horizon or check your watch. It's more soothing to pace, whistle, tap your foot, or rock back and forth on the hind legs of your chair.

Great lobbies and waiting rooms are designed to give strandees plenty of opportunities to engage in silly repetitive tasks: Count the lightbulbs in the chandeliers, figure out the pattern on the floor, or calculate the number of tiles on the wall.

Our internal clocks are sensitive to

In India, life is lived in the present tense.

changes of rhythms but also to temperature fluctuations. If we are hot, for example, we tend to underestimate the waiting time. It's wise, then, to stay away from drafty hallways. Better rub your upper arms when standing in line for a movie. Throw a shawl on your shoulders if you must wait by the phone. Sweat it out, as the saying goes.

Emotions can also tip the time scales this way or that way. Minutes feel like hours if you are made to sit in some dark governmental corridor, surrounded by the dour portraits of our founding fathers.

In contrast, researchers have found that gazing at smiling female faces can significantly abbreviate our perception of a wait. Strewn around your doctor's waiting room, those dog-eared fashion magazines are anti-time devices.

NOW OR NEVER

There are many ways to map out our imprecise perception of time. For centuries, people used lunar cycles, sundials, and church bells to sort out the events of their lives and keep them in chronological order. Eventually, in the twelfth century, Benedictine monks developed clocks to synchronize their communal activities.

But by far the most intriguing timekeeping invention was language.

The use of verbs reflects a culture's belief system regarding the nature of time. In English, for example, we say, "Your flight leaves in five hours" and "You will stop right now"—indiscriminately using the present tense to indicate a future action and the future tense to indicate a present one.

For us, the present moment is part of what's around the corner. Our grammar betrays the fact that we feel that "now" is only the prologue to more things to come.

In other languages, the forms of verbs emphasize other aspects of time, like whether an action will last or whether it is completed.

Less obsessed with what's going to happen next, these forms give users more room to stay in the moment—without feeling, as we do, that we must rush ahead in order to meet our impending fates.

You can change the way you feel about waiting simply by using the correct tense when you are stuck in a situation. No, your plane is not leaving in five hours—it *will* leave

There is a lot of emptiness in the universe—and it shows through.

in five hours. Give yourself five hours of free time rather than five hours of waiting for your flight to depart.

Waiting is not a prelude to the future. If anything, it is a prelude to the past.

The precious minutes, hours, or days we invest anticipating an event—the return of a friend, the birth of a child, the purchase of a house, or the last chapter of a book—make everything more memorable.

Take the time to wait. In doing so, you are manufacturing the stuff of your souvenirs.

Dawdle in the present tense. Give your future a past to remember.

How to Watch a Sunset

Doers that we are, we can't help but feel that the sun is like us—a busy celestial body running circles around the Earth. This false impression is a tenacious one, but we can resist it. The next time you watch a sunset, sit tight: Experience the Earth's majestic rotation. Here is how to do it.

1. Before dusk, face the sun as it nears the horizon. Notice how you assume that it is sinking. Remind yourself that this downward motion is an optical illusion.

2. Drive an imaginary stake through the sun and pin it to the sky. Make sure it doesn't budge.

3. Now watch the horizon climb gradually toward the sun. Imagine the ground shifting under your feet.

4. Give in to the feeling that the Earth is tilting backward in slow motion.

5. As the sun disappears, visualize your side of the planet rolling quietly into the twilight.

6. Congratulations. In the last ten minutes, you've done a ten-thousand-miles-per-hour backward somersault into the night.

"Knock on the sky and listen to the sound!" said the Zen master.

Ah! To do nothing—but be curious about everything.

You are five, six, or seven years old. You are playing quietly in your room—reading comics or giving your favorite doll a haircut. The house is silent, except for the dishwasher in its rinse cycle. A dog barks in the street. A sanitation truck whines in the distance. There is peace on earth.

Just then, your mother appears at the door.

"What are you doing?" she asks.

"Nothing," you reply absentmindedly. "I'm doing nothing."

Were she to insist, you would have to break the spell. Coming up with a grown-up explanation would disrupt the blissful sense of plenitude. For a child, doing nothing doesn't mean being inactive, it means doing something that doesn't have a name.

Today, you can recapture that moment of utter serenity simply by refusing to put a label on everything you do. Practice doing "nothing," whether you are busy in the kitchen, talking on the phone, or running late for an appointment.

You can make time for yourself by uncluttering your mind.

Aromatherapy: Massages or baths enhanced with essential oils from herbs, flowers, or fruits.

Balneotherapy: Water treatments that capitalize on the chemical properties of natural springs.

Catharsis: A sense of purification and spiritual renewal brought about by an artistic experience.

D'vekut: A Hasidic meditation practice that aims at creating a direct awareness of God.

Hydrotherapy: Revitalizing baths, showers, or soaks in warm or cold water.

Isometrics: A system of toning exercises in which opposing muscles push against each other.

Koan: A Zen mind puzzle that transcends logic and promotes intuitive enlightenment.

Mindfulness: A state of self-awareness based on relaxation and attention to the present moment.

Nirvana: A Buddhist state of beatitude that is characterized by the extinction of desire.

Prana: A yoga representation of the breath as the spiritual life force in the universe.

Rebirthing: A ritual that celebrates a spiritual regeneration similar to a second birth.

Reflexology: A Chinese healing technique that uses pressure points on feet, hands, and ears.

Samadhi: A Tibetan practice that produces intense concentration, called *one-pointedness of mind*.

Satori: A state of intuitive illumination triggered by Zen practice.

Tao: A Chinese principle that promotes nonassertive action in harmony with nature.

Thalassotherapy: Water treatments that use the therapeutic properties of seawater and seaweed.

Visualization: A relaxation technique that involves seeing images with your mind's eye.

Wu-Wei: The principle of spiritual nonaction in the Chinese philosophy of Tao.

Yoga: An Eastern practice that involves stretching, toning, breathing, and meditating.

Zen: A Japanese meditation practice that uses intuition and common sense in daily life.

Ackerman, Diane. *A Natural History of the Senses.* New York: Vintage Books, 1990.

Bachelard, Gaston. *La Dialectique de la durée.* Paris: Presses Universitaires de France, 1993.

Ban Breathnach, Sarah. *Simple Abundance.* New York: Warner Books, 1995.

Brillat-Savarin, Anthelme, translated and annotated by M. F. K. Fisher. *The Physiology of Taste.* San Francisco: North Point Press, 1986.

Cleary, Thomas. *Minding Mind.* Boston: Shambhala, 1995.

Gleick, James. *Chaos: Making a New Science.* New York: Viking Penguin, 1987.

Hawking, Stephen. *A Brief History of Time.* New York: Bantam Books, 1988.

Herrigel, Eugene. *Zen and the Art of Archery.* New York: Vintage Books, 1971.

Hoff, Benjamin. *The Tao of Pooh.* New York: Penguin Books, 1982.

Holland, Barbara. *Endangered Pleasures.* New York: Little, Brown and Co., 1995.

Katagiri, Dainin. *Returning to Silence.* Boston: Shambhala, 1988.

Kenkō, translated by Donald Keene. *Essays in Idleness.* New York: Columbia University Press, 1967.

Koren, Leonard. *Wabi-Sabi for Artists, Designers, Poets, and Philosophers.* Berkeley, Calif.: Stone Bridge Press, 1994.

Kundera, Milan, translated by Linda Asher. *Slowness.* New York: HarperCollins Publishers, 1996.

Lafargue, Paul. *The Right to Be Lazy.* New York: Gordon Press, 1972.

Lewis, Dennis. *The Tao of Natural Breathing.* San Francisco: Mountain Wind Publishing, 1996.

Matlin, Margaret. *Sensation and Perception.* Boston: Allyn and Bacon, Inc., 1988.

Merton, Thomas. *Raids on the Unspeakable.* New York: New Directions, 1964.

Merwin, W. S. *Writings to an Unfinished Accompaniment.* New York: Atheneum, 1980.

Nhat Hanh, Thich. *The Miracle of Mindfulness.* Boston: Beacon Press, 1975.

——. *Old Path White Clouds.* Berkeley, Calif.: Parallax Press, 1991.

Piquemal, Michel. *Paroles de Paresse.* Paris: Albin Michel, 1996.

Proust, Marcel. *Remembrance of Things Past and Other Essays.* New York: Random House, 1981.

Russell, Bertrand. *In Praise of Idleness and Other Essays.* New York: Routledge, Chapman & Hall, 1981.

Samuels, Mike and Nancy. *Seeing with the Mind's Eye.* New York: Random House, Bookworms Books, 1975.

Sartre, Jean-Paul, translated by Hazel Barnes. *Being and Nothingness.* New York: French & European Publications, 1993.

Schiller, David. *The Little Zen Companion.* New York: Workman Publishing, 1994.

Suzuki, Daisetz Teitaro. *Essays in Zen Buddhism.* York Beach, Maine: Samuel Weiser, 1985.

——. *The Zen Doctrine of No-Mind.* York Beach, Maine: Samuel Weiser, 1972

Thomas, Lewis. *The Lives of a Cell.* New York: Viking, 1984.

Thoreau, Henry David. *The Natural History Essays.* Salt Lake City: Gibbs M. Smith, Inc., 1984.

——. *Walden and Other Writings.* New York: Bantam Books, 1962.

Veblen, Thorstein. *The Theory of the Leisure Class.* New York: Dover Publications, Inc., 1994.

Watts, Allan. *Tao: The Watercourse Way.* New York: Pantheon, 1975.

——. *The Wisdom of Insecurity.* New York: Vintage Books, 1951.

Weil, Andrew. *Spontaneous Healing.* New York: Fawcett Columbine, 1995.

As a child growing up in California in the 1960s, I was blessed with an innate understanding of the meaning of doing nothing. Later I got busy and left behind that notion, but my photographs kept drawing me back to it. I traveled to Europe, India, Japan, Africa, and Egypt, always in search of images that captured the essence of serenity.

—ERICA LENNARD

Page 2: Man bathing in Takagarawa Onsen, Japan. Page 8: Black back, Paris, France. Pages 10–11: Garden bench in the Chateau du Marais, France. Page 13: Garden path in the Rousham Garden in England. Page 14: Waiting for the monsoon in Cochin, India. Pages 18–19: Claudia in Madeira. Page 21: Tree in Hampstead Heath, London, England. Page 22: Ann at Sally's house, in Bolinas, California. Page 25: Studio portrait of Kim in New York City. Pages 26–27: Garden of Jean Jacques Rousseau, Parc d'Ermenonville, France. Page 29: In the Tenryu-ji Temple, Kyoto, Japan. Page 30: Honen-In Temple, Kyoto, Japan. Page 32: Baby Neptune, rue de Rivoli, Paris. Pages 34–35: Claudia at the Reid's Hotel, Madeira. Page 37: Chez Irene and Giorgio, Provence. Page 38: Nymphenburg Gardens, Germany. Page 40: Sierra Leone, Africa. Pages 42–43: Neptune on Denis's desk, Paris. Page 45: Denis in his office in Paris. Page 47: Dancing legs, Petit Palais, Paris. Page 48: Lise in her loft, New York City. Pages 50–51: Thousand and One Nights, Cairo, Egypt. Page 52: Garden bed, Amber, India. Pages 56–57: Claudia in Madeira. Page 60: Women bathing, Takagarawa Onsen, Japan. Page 62: Galta, Rajasthan, India. Page 64: The White Rose, Kazuko's apartment, New York City. Pages 66–67: Buddhist temple food, Kyoto. Page 68: The market in Aix-en-Provence. Page 71: Claudia eating bread fruit in Madeira. Page 72: The fiftieth wedding anniversary of Joseph and Marie Jeanne Colomb, at Le Garde, Vauvenargues, France. Pages 74–75: Stormy day, Carmel, California. Page 77: Samba at the Sariska Wildlife Reserve, India. Page 79: Wedding preparations, New York City. Page 80: In the Rose Garden, Baden-Baden, Germany. Pages 82–83: Italian palazzo in Sicily. Page 85: Seated women, Jaiselmer, India. Page 87: Temple garden, Daisen-In, Kyoto. Page 88: Sunset in Marseilles, France, chez "Dede." Page 90: Lise, Isabel, and friends at "Madoo," in Sagaponack, Long Island.